T0039225

Prayers for Living

JANET L. STEINER

WESTBOW·
PRESS
A DIVISION OF THOMAS NELSON
& ZONDERVAN

Copyright © 2014 Janet L. Steiner.

All rights reserved. No part of this book may be used or reproduced by any means, graphic, electronic, or mechanical, including photocopying, recording, taping or by any information storage retrieval system without the written permission of the publisher except in the case of brief quotations embodied in critical articles and reviews.

WestBow Press books may be ordered through booksellers or by contacting:

WestBow Press
A Division of Thomas Nelson
1663 Liberty Drive
Bloomington, IN 47403
www.westbowpress.com
1 (866) 928-1240

Because of the dynamic nature of the Internet, any web addresses or links contained in this book may have changed since publication and may no longer be valid. The views expressed in this work are solely those of the author and do not necessarily reflect the views of the publisher, and the publisher hereby disclaims any responsibility for them.

Any people depicted in stock imagery provided by Thinkstock are models, and such images are being used for illustrative purposes only.
Certain stock imagery © Thinkstock.

ISBN: 978-1-4908-1830-6 (sc)
ISBN: 978-1-4908-1831-3 (e)

Library of Congress Control Number: 2013922447

Printed in the United States of America.

WestBow Press rev. date: 1/16/2014

Contents

Thanks to Pastor Daniel Haberkost and Charles Schnabel for proofreading the book. To my supportive Husband, David Steiner and his sugestions for the book. I give the Bible credit, in my life as well as this book, it has been support through hard times, it has illuminated my path. The Bible, the Word of God, Jesus who saves me.

CHAPTER 1

Prayers for Living

Matthew 5:10
Blessed are those who are persecuted for righteousness, for the kingdom of heaven belongs to them

There are Christians every day being oppressed by devil workers. What you cannot do is give up. Remember Jesus, Yeshua, left his place in heaven, came to earth humble, 100% man and 100% God, went to the cross and paid our price in full for every sin of all mankind of all time. There is nothing so bad that would ever separate us from the Love of God. The unforgivable sin is against the Holy Spirit, basically saying you reject this free wonderful gift of God paying the price for all your sin. If you do not accept Jesus, Yeshua as your Savior, that would be the only thing not forgivable. As long as you have breath you have the opportunity to accept this gift. When in the midst of this on-slot from the devil it is hard to keep your head straight, believe me I know, I have experienced such loud treacherous sounds and filth unimaginable. They have a way of placing inappropriate words and actions whenever and wherever possible. They would like nothing better than for you to end your life or for you to renounce your faith. They want to keep you from worship, reading the Bible, family and friends. What they do is beyond your control or wishes. This is not your battle, let God do battle for you. DO NOT LET THEM HAVE THEIR WAY! Reading the Bible will help you, it is not called a sword for no reason! These are a collection of scriptures that are praise to God and warfare made to strengthen you so you will be able to endure the on-slot from the adversary made into prayers.

<u>Wicked</u>-morally very bad : <u>evil</u> *a* : <u>fierce</u>, <u>vicious</u> *b* : disposed to or marked by mischief : <u>roguish</u> *a* : disgustingly unpleasant : <u>vile</u> *b* : causing or likely to cause harm, distress, or trouble

Some scriptures using the word wicked also say man, but that is also the lot laid up for anything wicked that comes against Shaddai (God).

Yes humans can be wicked, give your life over to GOD, your thoughts and desires can change. You can find yourself wanting to be more like the One who paid for your price of sin. You need to break off of your life the old ways, finding your life lighter. The more baggage from your own life you can get rid of, the better, get rid of anger, malice, lust, pride, selfishness, guilt and any negative emotion or feelings. These if held on to will sicken the soul, by going to GOD for help and letting go of them there is such a release. And remember

Yeshua Paid for your price, your home is heaven. Now what we should be cultivating is the fruits of the spirit.

Galatians 5:22-26
World English Bible (WEB)

22 But the fruit of the Spirit is love, joy, peace, patience, kindness, goodness, faith, 23 gentleness, and self-control. Against such things there is no law. 24 Those who belong to Christ have crucified the flesh with its passions and lusts. 25 If we live by the Spirit, let's also walk by the Spirit. 26 Let's not become conceited, provoking one another, and envying one another.

Created or heavenly beings on the other hand understand things that humans cannot and knew better than to do such wicked immoral actions. Do not pity or forgive any of their behavior!

Reflections on my Experience

Abba's voice=Yeshua (Jesus) =Word of God

Ruah HaKodesh (Holy Spirit)-No record of a voice that I know of

Yeshua- Only needs 1 voice, each Christian has the indwelling of the Ruah HaKodesh(Holy Spirit) and take Communion, Yeshua(Jesus)

body and blood taken inwardly but Yeshua(Jesus) has 1 voice, can communicate to any Christian.

Yeshua knows your heart and knows you are a Christian, Why wouldn't He be able to tell who you are, knows your deeds and can tell the difference between yours and another creations deeds.

There is one Yeshua (Jesus) not thousands, He is present everywhere and does dwell inside of me and other Christians. Be still seated at the Father's Right Hand and never be divided against himself.

Abba is a fair judge and wants the Best for You.

Abba, Yeshua, Ruah HaKodesh in Christians or anywhere is all powerful at all times and fully able to save, separate you from the devil worker, fully able to Do, Act, Move as HE Wills. If HE decides to see you through it you are no more or less loved than the one who received the miracle.

People cannot be divided Body-Soul on opposite sides.

Soul=who you are, personality cannot divide and have a different voice and talk to you.

Demon -Joy and life drain, basically of anything good or positive.

*acts, then talks, trying to get "permission" but GOD is his Boss, not us.

*The demon is always subject to the will of the Creator (Abba, Yeshua, Ruah HaKodesh).

No matter what Abba is capable to save and wants the Best for His Children! It says in Scripture that Abba wants our life to be full of Joy, that does not mean we won't have problems, but more do not need to be created.

*Abba can heal and still does, just because the devil worker can mask your healing does not mean the healing is not still there!

You are covered with garments of salvation, a robe of righteousness, covered in Yeshua's glory. That is how much your Heavenly Father loves you!

Yours now as a Christians and member of heaven, just not see-able by human eyes on earth. Our sins are paid for now, we have the indwelling now, members of heaven now. Just as in Adam, the body is viewed as sinful because of the one act of disobedience. In Jesus, our bodies are viewed as righteous because of the one act of obedience, HE took all sins of all time so we take on His righteousness.

Righteous- made right by GOD, pure and sinless because our sins, even the ones we haven't done yet are paid for in full.

The Sinful ones made sinless because Jesus took our sins as his own on the cross. So our bodies are not viewed as sinful because of the sinless one. Covered in Yeshua's Glory.

The demon will try to shame you with your own body but God does not make junk! Love- something that the demon twists for his purpose.

A Father's Love for his Children they do not want to understand.

There is much pain and suffering in the world, I don't think this side of heaven we will ever really understand. I know Satan and his crew are alive and well and there is plenty of evidence in this world of that. Our home is not this world, we are here just a short time, and then we will go Home to Heaven, until then let's do what we can to further God's Kingdom. We show who we belong to with our deeds while here because they flow from a changed heart.

So let's follow the perfect example, Yeshua, Jesus.

Let us support one another in prayer, lend a helping hand, say a positive word to one who needs it, and when words will not do, give a hug that speaks beyond words. Let's do the will of our Father in Heaven.

CHAPTER 2

Miracles do Happen Now! Janet's Life Stories.

This is some events of my life as I can remember. I have certainly kept my angels of protection busy. Thank the Good Lord that he loves and cares for us so much.

I have been hearing a voice that speaks awful things, not of me, trying to break down my faith in Jesus, my Savior. It has been over a year ago when this started, before my TIA (mini stroke), the voices, and the reason for my TIA (mini stroke). People that go through this are not weak Christians, or any different than you. We all as human beings go through in our daily lives the full gambit of emotions and hard times occasionally, on the contrary, it is my faith in Jesus which got me through an impossible situation. I was hearing things and very depressed. That in itself is enough to make a person very uneasy. Sure I was being attacked by the enemy, I took 2 whole bottles of strong pain medicine with a full bottle of red wine and went to bed without my CPAP Machine. I did it because I felt I had no fight left and wanted to protect my family. You see, the evil voice said anyone told would die, an empty threat I Know, but in the middle of confusion I wasn't sure. I have a serious problem which causes me to stop breathing an enormous amount of times at night. I wanted to go to that beautiful light that I remember, that is God's presence. This light knows everything, good and bad about you, everything, and loves you anyways. Pure Love, Joy and Peace I never wanted to leave, but have more to do here on earth. I had no logical reason to expect anything but reaching that light. I was told I would not be able to reach the light by a kind, gentle but firm voice. I also heard a voice that was gentle, kind and loving, but sometimes stated things firmly. I should of listened, but I didn't. I know who loves me and would direct me the correct direction, God would. I believe in my worst times HE was there beside me, No, HE was carrying me! Going to sleep without that machine with that much in me I know that is a miracle from The LORD himself! The next thing I remember is responding to people by looking at them, not able to move my body. A couple of days have passed since that night I took the pills. Liver has a toxic amount in it. I had to fight to get back. I was given 2 new pills that would help in quieting things down. I know it is God who gave me this doctor to help me and God working in my life through the medicine helping me, God miraculously helping me even though I occasionally still have the adversary close by and aware of it. God who will never leave or forsake me. There is nothing in your life that will shock or surprise The Creator of all. There is nothing in your life terrible enough for Him to forsake you. You would have to reject Him for that to happen! When God says He will never leave you, He means it!

This happened the summer after the first time through 2nd grade. I was at a family reunion, the meal was over and a few of us went to play in the park. The park has a hill, the pavilion we use was at the bottom of the hill. I decided to go to the tallest slide in the park. It has cement below it all around the base. I climbed the ladder and had decided to try something I saw some older kids do. They would slide down just on the butt with the legs held off the slide. I got up and sat down ready to try this, lost my balance and fell head first on the cement! The next I can vaguely remember is being in the hospital, severe concussion. Time went by and I got better enough to come home, lost my memory, I asked the nurse if she was sure this was my family. I am positive that this is a miracle that I lived through such a severe injury and that I did not have any other damage. Hitting head first on cement and not breaking the neck and becoming paralyzed or to tell the truth, I look back and see that it could of just as easily taken my life right there. I estimated it to be about a 8 foot slide-drop head first on cement as a 2nd grade child.

Growing up I lived 1 block from the train tracks, the better part of town was far on the other side of town. Grade school was hard for me. The others in my class did not like me. In class they would kick me and after school walking home they would gang up on and beat me. Some of the time the older kids would join in the beating. Every evening in my room I would talk to GOD about it and about anything else that was on my mind. I felt strongly He was right there beside me. It was from HIM I got to treat them with kindness even though they weren't easy to be nice to. Every day I would try to be kind and treat them nicely. Every day after school the same, a beating. Some had steel toed shoes, some had heavy pins at the end at their toe to prick with. They would work at me until they got me down to the ground, or until I would manage to get away and run off. The times knocked to the ground they would kick me and spit on me. This happened all through grade school, but stopped before 7th grade. The last one I got a surprise. Someone from class, a quiet boy, was walking on the sidewalk on the other side of the street. Seeing I was about to be overtaken again he called out to them defending me. That made them angry. They went after him instead. He told me to run, I did. It was many years later, I was married adult. I happen to meet up with one of those of my class who participated in those beatings. He recalled that part of his childhood and it reminded him of Jesus. He placed himself as one who rejected Jesus. He told me that it was something GOD used to bring him to faith. In all of my grade school beatings none broke a single bone. That was a miracle of GOD. The only reason I can see of that is God's wonderful hand of protection.

There is a bone, though, that was broken, by a hole in the ground in my own yard, broke my foot in three places. Lived with it that way not set from grade school time all the way to an adult. My left foot would be crooked, heel straight but front part of the foot directed outward. I was at a messianic service, afterward three women came to me and said "you know you don't have to stand for it. Let me pray for you." They sat me down and prayed. My body felt like I was in a furnace from the inside out. I looked at my foot after prayer and it was a lot straighter. Went to bed and the next morning my foot was completely straight. I now cannot even put the foot in the same position if I try. Heavenly Father is still in the healing business! Another Miracle straight from HIS HAND.

Tippy was our family dog, a collie and my friend. My dad was very close to him, we had neighbors who continually would shoot across the road with bb guns and other types also. They seem to wait so as not to get caught shooting in town. One day my dad was on the roof and in the tree only a couple feet away was a protected bird they shot right out of the tree! That was shocking to us. Our family dog latter got sick. Dad told me he had lead poisoning from too many bb's in his head. I saw how deeply hurt my dad was and I was filled with anger. That anger at them bottled up was making me sick inside. I decided to take it to The Lord. HE helped me let go and I in prayer forgave them of what they did and felt such a release! If you turn to the Creator of All with what anger is sickening your soul and truly ask the LORD, "Lord, this is too much for me to deal with help me to forgive those who have wronged me, I want to let go of this burden. HE will help you. I then was able to say that I forgave them, and let go of that pain in my heart. I never approached them with it, I did not think they would understand, or think they needed to be forgiven. It is important to completely forgive from the heart, HE will help you through like HE did with me.

I had outside cats, one was an orange tabby, Charlie was feeding one day and was bitten by him, he never had his rabies shot and that day he acted quite strange, he usually was gentle cat and this was very out of character. Could not find him afterward and the scare of rabies had me schedule to start the painful series of shots with no assurance I would live through it. The day I was to receive the first in the series of shots, here comes Charlie a full week latter perfectly normal, no signs of any rabies. At that point I contacted the veterinarian and he stated there was no need for me to go through the shots. The cat would have been very sick or dead by that point in time. Another of Heavenly Father's miracles.

David was outside mowing the lawn and decided to try and mow the milk-house hill with the riding mower. He went up, the mower overturned trapping his foot under with the blade. The mower's safety fails, and still the mower blade stops! The mower did not, with his foot trapped he was dragged all the way to the row of pine trees. A hard blow on his back running into the tree dislodged him. It looked miraculously like a small surface scratch, we went on vacation to Florida. David's small scratch fast turned to a very smelly and painful swollen leg he could barely stand. Rushed him home and found it was gangrene, we were at Aultman Hospital and he was very serious, I was not sure he would survive, then I thought he might have a chance, but survive without a leg. ABBA was not only able to have him live, but also with both legs fully functional. What an Awesome

GOD we serve! I would not know what I would do without my loving supportive husband. Thank You LORD!

I was filling the stove with wood and one piece of burning wood was falling out. I used my gloved hands to put it back in twice without even the gloves having a burn spot. Thank You LORD!

I was in the top floor of the barn and the floor under me gave way. One foot completely went through and I knew I was soon to land on the cement floor of the first floor which had a layer of old hay, as I thought. The next I was landing on the wood floor of the same level beside the hole! That is impossible but with God all things are possible! We have a Loving GOD we serve, Thank You for the Miracles in my life! These are but a few, there are more HE has provided for me. I am truly grateful we have such a Loving Father who provides what we need at times even without us asking!

I remember once being in the presence of the Pure Light which knows everything about you, everything you have done and loves you anyways just as you are. Pure Love, Joy and Peace. The Light goes right through you. Such a feeling of complete acceptance, joy, love and peace, I never wanted to leave. I was a bit disappointed when I awoke, but I knew I needed to be here yet.

CHAPTER 3

Psalm 23 with personal explanation

You can pray these scriptures, or read them aloud, praying scriptures with praise and warfare against your enemy will help.

1 The LORD is my shepherd; I shall not want.

*Because the LORD is my protection, my Teacher, my heavenly Father he supplies all my needs and I lack in nothing.

2 He makes me lie down in green pastures. He leads me beside still waters. 3 He restores my soul.

*He takes me to a perfect place of safety where there is enough of food, enough of an area to rest and the best place to refresh me when thirsty.

He leads me in paths of righteousness for his name's sake.

*Jesus of Nazareth, my Savior has paid my price in full and for his sake I am guided on in the right path.

4 Even though I walk through the valley of the shadow of death, I will fear no evil, for you are with me; your rod and your staff, they comfort me.

*I do not take up Residency in the darkest valley, enemy's area, where I am sure I am surrounded by the enemy, with GOD beside me, he will never leave you or forsake you, I walk through it. The evil there does not frighten, you TRUST your Shepherd, He is not slow to stop the enemy from causing any harm. Here is a promise, the valley of the shadow of death where the enemy seems to be so near, will not be your whole life, he sees you through it, to the other side, past it. He always does, it just might not seem like it at the time.

5 You prepare a table before me in the presence of my enemies; you anoint my head with oil; my cup overflows.

*I have a banquet spread before me, and eat in safety with my enemies around watching, they can see, but cannot harm. Kings, prophets and priests were anointed, I am a Child of the Heavenly Father!

A Cup overflowing, Our Joy should be overflowing as the blessing of GOD, that is what He wants for us!

6 Surely goodness and mercy shall follow me all the days of my life, and I shall dwell in the house of the LORD forever.

*The Heavenly Father shows me his goodness and love all the days of my life. Something the enemy cannot understand, a Father's Love! I know He will not leave me unprotected. Sometimes it feels like you are unprotected, don't believe it. Everyone goes through the valley of the shadow of death sometimes. I know I have a place in HIS HOUSE Forever!

Amen

CHAPTER 4

Prayers

Prayers for living

These prayers and scriptures are meant to help the Christian struggling with emotional, mental and physical assaults from the enemy, when battling through sorrow, pain, feelings of abandonment by GOD, loneliness, you feel defeated. Turn to scripture and prayer. God has not abandoned you! You can be reassured, comforted, maybe even uplifted.

I myself have battled through a full gambit of these and what got me through it is prayer, music and scripture, the friendship of my Pastors and my devoted husband. We are given these because our Heavenly Father understood we would need them, when going through the tough times of life hang on to them, it will help. There were times that it got so bad I would turn on Christian music and turn it loud, that would help, sometimes scripture, I have on my phone a version that reads it aloud to you, that helps in bad times, and just talking to

GOD, there is nothing he can't help you through! I can do all things through God who strengthens me!

P.S. Yeshua and Jesus are the same person.

Abba means Father

Loved One's Troubled Times

Abba,
I see my loved one in such pain and anguish and feel helpless to do something about it. I have such mixed emotions of anger and care for my loved one and wish there was something I could do. I know what I am tempted to do would not be good for either of us, Holy Father we need help. I so need to feel your shalom, I need to feel your presence guiding our lives. I know you haven't left us but we are feeling mighty alone here. Give me direction for the way we are to go, Protection from the evil all about, uplift our spirits, and help us make it past this troubled time. In Yeshua's Name,
Amen

Abba,
There are so many hurting people around the world going through such terrible times that need your support, need to feel loved that feel they don't deserve to be loved and can't forgive themselves, help

them make the first step in forgiving themselves because you love them anyways, just the way they are. Help them accept the free gift, your love which paid the price for us.

In Yeshua's Name

Amen

Confusion

Abba,

My heart feels sorrowful and I am in confusion, Lord clear my confused mind, I know you will never leave or forsake us and that you are with us always but I am not understanding why this is going on so long, Lord help bring understanding back to me. Guard me I pray from the attacks of the enemy, I want to pray for the rest of my church family feeling such attacks as these, Lord Guard our minds from evil thoughts, our lips from speaking evil, our bodies from affliction and pain, Help us feel not so separated from you, and fill us with your peace that is beyond our understanding here on earth.

In Yeshua's Name

Amen

Abba,

My mind is all jumbled up with confusing thought, help me. I am your child. I have been crucified with Christ, and it is no longer I that live,

but Christ living in me. That life which I now live in the flesh, I live by faith in the Son of God, who loved me, and gave himself up for me and because of Messiah and his wonderful works, we say For though we walk in the flesh, we don't wage war according to the flesh; for the weapons of our warfare are not of the flesh, but mighty before God to the throwing down of strongholds, throwing down imaginations and every high thing that is exalted against the knowledge of God, and bringing every thought into captivity to the obedience of Christ; and being in readiness to avenge all disobedience, when your obedience will be made full. Straighten my confused thoughts, remove any way in me that is offensive. In Yeshua's Name
Amen

The Lord's Prayer

Our Father in heaven,
Hallowed be your name. Your kingdom come. Your will be done on earth as it is in heaven. Give us this day our daily bread. And forgive us our debts, as we forgive our debtors. And do not lead us into temptation, but deliver us from the evil one. For yours is the kingdom and the power and the glory forever.
Amen.

Comfort

God,
Blessed be the God and Father of our Lord Yeshua the Messiah, the Father of mercies and God of all comfort; who comforts us in all our affliction, that we may be able to comfort those who are in any affliction, through the comfort with which we ourselves are comforted by God. The LORD, he it is who does go before you; he will be with you, he will not fail you, neither forsake you; don't be afraid, neither be dismayed, for I am with you; says The Lord, don't be dismayed, for I am your God; I will strengthen you; yes, I will help you; yes, I will uphold you with the right hand of my righteousness. Thank You for your Word of Truth. In Yeshua's Name,
Amen

Peace

Dear Father in Heaven,
In Isaiah 26:3 it says you will keep him in perfect shalom, whose mind is stayed on you; because he trusts in you. Lord I am in need of your perfect Shalom, Protect my mind from the adversaries work. I do Trust in you, you are the only way to heaven, The Truth, The life and The Way.
In Yeshua's Name
Amen

Forgiveness

Lord,
There is someone that I cannot seem to forgive and this is making me sick inside. Help me to let go of what I am holding against my neighbor for in your scripture it says if you forgive others their trespasses, your Heavenly Father will also forgive you. I will bless the Lord, O my soul, and I will forget not his benefits, who forgives all iniquities, who heals all my diseases!
In Yeshua's Name
Amen

Abba,
I know that all have sinned and fall short of the glory of God. That you demonstrate Your righteousness in the present time, so that he would be just and the justifier of the one who lives because of Jesus' faithfulness, a person is declared righteous by faith apart from the works of the law. I thank you for your word. May I not loose sight of truth, Heaven is my home! I pray in Yeshua's Name.
Amen

Salvation

Dear Father in Heaven,
I am a sinner of need of the precious work that Jesus did for me on the cross. He who knew no sin took on all the sin of all time so I could

have heaven as my home. In Romans 10: 8-9 says The word is near you, in your mouth, and in your heart; that is, the word of faith, which we preach: that if you will confess with your mouth the Lord Yeshua/Jesus, and believe in your heart that God raised him from the dead, you will be saved. I now Confess Yeshua/Jesus Is Messiah, Lord of my Life and he is now seated at the right hand of God the Father. I believe because of this precious gift God has given me, heaven is now my home. Help me Lord to live a life that shows who I belong to. In Yeshua's Name
Amen

Abba, Heavenly Father,
You are rich in mercy, because of Your great love with which he loved us, even though we were dead in transgressions, made us alive together with Christ—by grace I am saved!-and he raised us up with him and seated us with him in the heavenly realms in Christ Jesus, to demonstrate in the coming ages the surpassing wealth of his grace in kindness toward us in Christ Jesus. For by grace I am saved through faith, and this is not from ourselves, it is the gift of God; it is not from works, so that no one can boast. But now in Christ Jesus you who used to be far away have been brought near by the blood of Christ. For he is our peace, you reconciled me to God through the cross, by which the hostility has been killed. So then we are no longer foreigners and non-citizens, but we are fellow citizens with the saints and members of God's household, because you have been built on the foundation of the apostles and prophets, with Christ Jesus himself as

the cornerstone. Your grace and mercy truly has no end! Praise be to God! I pray in Yeshua's Name.

Amen

Abba, Father,

I am glad you love us and take us in as your own children, Lord I look to Your Word, in it, it states- For all who are led by the Spirit of God are the sons of God. For you did not receive the spirit of slavery leading again to fear, but you received the Spirit of adoption, by whom we cry, *"Abba,* Father." The Spirit himself bears witness to our spirit that we are God's children. And if children, then heirs namely, heirs of God and also fellow heirs with Christ—if indeed we suffer with him so we may also be glorified with him. For I consider that our present sufferings cannot even be compared to the coming glory that will be revealed to us. The Spirit helps us in our weakness, for we do not know how we should pray, but the Spirit himself intercedes for us with inexpressible groaning. And he who searches our hearts knows the mind of the Spirit, because the Spirit intercedes on behalf of the saints according to God's will. And we know that all things work together for good for those who love God, who are called according to his purpose, we have complete victory through him who loved us! For I am convinced that neither death, nor life, nor angels, nor heavenly rulers, nor things that are present, nor things to come, nor powers, nor height, nor depth, nor anything else in creation will be able to separate us from the love of God in Christ Jesus our Lord. Your word speaks truth, gives hope, directs

us to The Way The Truth and The Life in Him we can say heaven is our home. Thanks be to God. In Yeshua's Name
Amen

Heavenly Father,
Yeshua has destroyed the works of the devil, I am subject to God and resist the devil, you say he will flee from me. Yeshua said I tell you the solemn truth, everyone who practices sin is a slave of sin. The slave does not remain in the family forever, but the son remains forever. So if the son sets you free, you will be really free. I look forward to seeing you, Lord, and the life to come, in heaven. Hallelujah! I pray in Yeshua's Name.
Amen

Lord,
I am glad you choose to dwell with us, I look forward to the time you will wipe away every tear from the eyes and death will be no more You make all things new, you are the Alef and the Tav, the Beginning and the End. Yet you choose to abide with us and save us from sin and open heaven to any who believe in your Son. Thank You, I pray in Yeshua's Name.
Amen

Repentance

Lord,
You say all flesh will see God's salvation bring forth fruits worthy of repentance. Every tree therefore that doesn't bring forth good fruit is cut down, and thrown in the fire. I am sorry for my sins Lord, and I have the forgiveness, let my life bring forth good fruit for your kingdom. Lord.
In Yeshua's Name
Amen

Father in Heaven,
I have sinned and fallen short of your glory of God, but I am truly sorry for what I have done and seek your forgiveness. Help me to live a life following the Perfect example, Yeshua/Jesus who died for me.
In Yeshua's Name
Amen

Healing

Abba,
You are mighty and I will praise you. Your thoughts are far above our thoughts yet you care so much for us who cannot possibly understand your Mighty Hand. My health is not very good, I do not understand why I am so afflicted, but I look at the cross and see how much

you care for us. Let me be able to say but as for me, I know that my Redeemer lives. In the end, he will stand upon the earth. After my skin is destroyed, then in my flesh shall I see God, Whom I, even I, shall see on my side. My eyes shall see, and not as a stranger. My heart is consumed within me. Yes surely, God will not do wickedly, neither will the Almighty pervert justice.

In Yeshua's Name

Amen

Abba,

My body is plagued with ailments, Guide my doctors to have the right diagnosis and guide their hands in healing. You, Lord are the Great Physician and I Trust in You. I know your Name is above any name that the doctors can say over me. It doesn't matter what it is you can make me well. Heal me and I will be healed.

In Yeshua's Name

Amen

Holy Father,

I am sick and tired of being sick and tired. Many are my afflictions, I ask the Lord to deliver me out of them. Your scripture says, for I will restore health to you, and your wounds I will heal, Lord restore health once more I pray,

In Yeshua's Name

Amen

Heavenly Father,

I will serve the Lord my God and I ask for you to bless my bread an my water and take sickness away from me as the scripture says, I trust in you Lord with all my heart, your word says do not lean on your own understanding in all your ways acknowledge him, and he will make straight your paths. Be not wise in your own eyes; fear the Lord, and turn away from evil. It will be healing to your flesh and refreshment to your bones. I do acknowledge you Lord and try to follow your ways. I need healing and refreshment, Lord take sickness away from me.

In Yeshua's Name

Amen

$$$ Problems

Abba,

I am in debt, owing more than I can pay. I need help, Holy Father your scripture says your Father knows what you need before you ask him, no good thing does he withhold. I am asking for supernatural help in this matter, Father.

In Yeshua's Name

Amen

Sleep

Holy Father,
I am troubled and this is showing up in my life as sleeplessness. Give a restful sleep, I pray The LORD is my shepherd; I shall not want. He makes me lie down in green pastures. He leads me beside still waters. He restores my soul. He leads me in paths of righteousness for his name's sake. Even though I walk through the valley of the shadow of death, I will fear no evil, for you are with me; your rod and your staff, they comfort me. You prepare a table before me in the presence of my enemies; you anoint my head with oil; my cup overflows. Surely goodness and mercy shall follow me all the days of my life, and I shall dwell in the house of the LORD forever. Calm my restlessness, give me your shalom. In shalom I will both lie down and sleep; for you alone, O Lord, make me dwell in safety.
In Yeshua's Name
Amen

Holy Father,
Sleepless nights or nights with little sleep I seem to have abundantly. Give restful sleep, I trust in your word which says He will cover you with his pinions, and under his wings you will find refuge; his faithfulness is a shield and buckler. You will not fear the terror of the night, nor the pestilence that stalks in darkness, nor the destruction that wastes at noonday. A thousand may fall at your side, ten thousand at your right hand, but it will not come near you.

Thank You Abba for caring so much for your children, for the Lord God is sun and shield; the Lord bestows favor and honor. No good thing does he withhold from those who walk uprightly and I will draw near with a true heart in full assurance of faith, with heart sprinkled clean with the blood of Yeshua from an evil conscience, body washed with pure water. Sanctified through the offering of the body of Yeshua, once for all.

In Yeshua's Name

Amen

Buckler-a small round shield either carried or worn on the arm. A means of protection, a defense.

Lord,

Your word says if you lie down you will not be afraid; when you lie down sleep will be sweet. You will forget your misery; you will remember it as waters that have passed away, and you will feel secure, because there is hope; you will lie down and none will make you afraid. Abba, when I lie down let me feel secure and let my sleep be sweet. In peace I will both lie down and sleep; for you alone, O Lord, make me dwell in safety.

Amen

Heavenly Father,

You are a shield about me, my glory, and the lifter of my head. I cried aloud to the Lord and he answered me from his holy hill. I lay down

and slept; I woke again, for the Lord sustained me. In my trouble let me not forget, you sustain me and give me rest. Let my sleep be sweet and arise fully rested.
In Yeshua's Name
Amen

Strength

Lord,
I love your Name the Name of the Lord is a strong tower; the righteous run to Him and are safe. I know I am righteous only by what you have done for me, you give the weary rest and strengthen the weak. I am weary and tired, give rest and strengthen me for what lies ahead. I pray in Yeshua's Name
Amen

Abba,
You say even the hairs on your head are all numbered. Do not be afraid; you are more valuable than many sparrows. Don't be afraid, for I am with you! Don't be frightened, for I am your God! I strengthen you—yes, I help you—yes, I uphold you with my saving right hand! Look, all who were angry at you will be ashamed and humiliated; your adversaries will be reduced to nothing and perish. When you will look for your opponents, you will not find them; your enemies will be reduced to absolutely nothing. For I am the LORD your God,

the one who takes hold of your right hand, who says to you, 'Don't be afraid, I am helping you.' I praise you for your mighty works. I praise your Name! I pray in Yeshua's Name.

Amen

Protection

Abba

This is a fallen world and we are a fallen people but I also know I am a child of GOD, and I know that you have paid for all my sins of my whole life, I am redeemed. Protect me from the effects of the adversary I pray and give me your peace, strengthen me so I can face what is ahead for me. I so need your presence, Abba, let me feel you with me as I know you are.

In Yeshua's Name

Amen

Lord,

I will sing about loyalty and justice! To you, O LORD, I will sing praises! I will walk in the way of integrity. When will you come to me? Praise the LORD, O my soul! O LORD my God, you are magnificent. You are robed in splendor and majesty. I will sing to the LORD as long as I live; I will sing praise to my God as long as I exist! May my thoughts be pleasing to him! I will rejoice in the LORD. May sinners

disappear from the earth, and the wicked vanish! Praise the Lord, O my soul! Praise the Lord! I pray in Yeshua's Name.
Amen

Abba,

O Lord, you examine me and know. You know when I sit down and when I get up; even from far away you understand my motives. You carefully observe me when I travel or when I lie down to rest; you are aware of everything I do. Certainly my tongue does not frame a word without you, O Lord, being thoroughly aware of it. You squeeze me in from behind and in front; you place your hand on me. Your knowledge is beyond my comprehension; it is so far beyond me, I am unable to fathom it. Where can I go to escape your spirit? Where can I flee to escape your presence? If I were to ascend to heaven, you would be there. If I were to sprawl out in Sheol, there you would be. If I were to fly away on the wings of the dawn, and settle down on the other side of the sea, even there your hand would guide me, your right hand would grab hold of me. If I were to say, "Certainly the darkness will cover me, and the light will turn to night all around me," even the darkness is not too dark for you to see, and the night is as bright as day; darkness and light are the same to you. Certainly you made my mind and heart; you wove me together in my mother's womb. I will give you thanks because your deeds are awesome and amazing. You knew me thoroughly; my bones were not hidden from you, when I was made in secret and sewed together in the depths of the earth. Your eyes saw me when I was inside the womb. All the days ordained

for me were recorded in your scroll before one of them came into existence. How difficult it is for me to fathom your thoughts about me, O God! How vast is their sum total! If I tried to count them, they would outnumber the grains of sand. Even if I finished counting them, I would still have to contend with you. If only you would kill the wicked, O God! O LORD, do I not hate those who hate you, and despise those who oppose you? I absolutely hate them, they have become my enemies! Examine me, and probe my thoughts! Test me, and know my concerns! Get away from me, you violent men! They rebel against you and act deceitfully; your enemies lie. O LORD, do I not hate those who hate you, and despise those who oppose you? I absolutely hate them, they have become my enemies! Examine me, and probe my thoughts! Test me, and know my concerns! See if there is any wicked way in me, and lead me in the everlasting way. I pray in Yeshua's Name.
Amen

Heavenly Father,
Lift up a standard against the enemy that has come in like a flood. Abba, you say in scripture I give unto you power to tread on serpents and scorpions, and over all the power of the enemy and nothing shall by any means hurt you and the weapons of our warfare are not carnal, but mighty through God to the pulling down of strongholds, casting down imaginations, and every high thing that exults itself against the knowledge of God and bringing into captivity every thought to the obedience of Christ. I am a child of God and greater is He that is in

me than that in the world. Yeshua came and was made manifest that He might destroy the works of the devil and His last words were, It is Finished. Halleluiah, Praise the Lord!

In Yeshua's Name

Amen

Heavenly Father,

Protect me from the attacks from the adversary, the devil and his workers. Protect my mind from confusion, my body from the attacks these things bring on. Guard my lips from evil speech, Do not let me loose who I am in these attacks, Let me not be moved from my faith in you, Holy Father. I do say to these devil workers attacking me, I rebuke you in Yeshua's Name, You Have to Leave. Father protect all who I come in contact with from any attacks. I cover my family with the Blood of Yeshua, protect my house, my property and all I own Abba, from the adversary, I pray in Yeshua's Name.

Amen

Abba,

Plead my cause, O Lord, with them that strive with me, fight against them that fight against me, come with vengeance, even God with recompense, Come and save me.

In Yeshua's Name

Amen

Troubled Times

Holy Father,
This is a strange path I am on, trying to do your will with an adversary present. Please direct me in what to do, Lord make it obvious. I pray.
In Yeshua's Name
Amen

Heavenly Father,
I know my righteousness comes only by you and what you have done for me. Yeshua has paid for my sins and removed them, even the ones I have not done yet that is in my life ahead of me. I hold fast to my righteousness, and will not let it go. My heart shall not reproach me so long as I live. Let my enemy be as the wicked. Let him who rises up against me be as the unrighteous. I broke the jaws of the unrighteous and plucked the prey out of his teeth. By The Name above all names- Yeshua! Praise your Holy Name!
Amen

God,
Help me to accept the things I can't change, give me the courage to change what I can, and the wisdom to know the difference, and I can do all things through Christ who strengthens me.
In Yeshua's Name
Amen

Abba,

In this time of affliction I turn to you for help, Lord, I do feel so separated from you right now, help me to withstand. Strengthen me, Help me understand, because right now, Father, I can't seem to, I do need you so desperately, remove my enemies far from me I pray. Put a shield of protection around me to guard me against these on-slots from the enemy, I pray for angels protection to guard my life, Lord let me not forget how easy you make it for me to be accepted in heaven with open arms, Belief in My Messiah, Yeshua /Jesus who Paid for my price. In Yeshua's Name
Amen

Heavenly Father,

Oh that you would bless me and enlarge my border, and that your hand might be with me, and that you would keep me from harm so that it might not bring me pain! My soul magnifies the Lord, and my spirit rejoices in God my Savior, for he has looked on the humble estate of his servant, he who is mighty has done great things for me, and holy is his name. I thank you that you have heard me. I knew that you always hear me. I thank you that you will not leave or forsake us. God, be merciful to me, a sinner!' To you, O LORD, I lift up my soul. O my God, in you I trust; let me not be put to shame; let not my enemies exult over me. My heart exults in the LORD; my strength is exalted in the LORD. My mouth derides my enemies, because I rejoice in your salvation. There is none holy like the LORD; there is none besides you; there is no rock like our God.

Please remember me and please strengthen me. For this reason I bow my knees before the Father, from whom every family in heaven and on earth is named, that according to the riches of his glory he may grant me to be strengthened with power through his Spirit in my inner being, How great are his signs, how mighty his wonders! His kingdom is an everlasting kingdom, and his dominion endures from generation to generation. Please make my Journey, walk in life, successful, productive for your kingdom. O LORD, O Lord, do I fear. In the midst of the years revive it; in the midst of the years make it known; in wrath Lord, remember me in mercy. Lord, if you are willing, you can make me clean. Lord, heal me and I will be completely well; rescue me and I will be perfectly safe. You are the one I praise! O LORD God of heaven, the great and awesome God who keeps covenant and steadfast love with those who love him and keep his commandments, let your ear be attentive and your eyes open, to hear the prayer of your servant that I now pray before you. I called out to the LORD, out of my distress, and he answered me; out of the belly of Sheol I cried, and you heard my voice. O LORD, there is none like you to help, between the mighty and the weak. Help us, O LORD our God, for we rely on you, and in your name. Though our iniquities testify against us, act, O LORD, for your name's sake. Give your servant therefore an understanding mind…that I may discern between good and evil. Nevertheless, not my will, but yours, be done. In Yeshua's Name,

Amen

Heavenly Father,

I do not think I like what I am very much, I have been stuck in survival mode for so long there is parts of me I do not like. Please minister to me, I am hurt and do not have anywhere else I would want to turn to. With this evil thing lurking around causing havoc in my life I cannot seem to shake. I know the One who has paid for all my sins in full, but this evil seems to be asking for another payment. I look to you for help, for protection, for guidance, for wisdom, for the saving of my life, for nourishment in the word, for uplifting, for hope for a future, for joy, for peace, even the time of praise and prayer when you call us to worship is something that fills my spirit and lifts me, helping me to deal with another week. Please, take this evil far from me and mend my broken heart.

In Yeshua's Name

Amen

Lord,

I love your scriptures and speak them to you. I lift up my eyes to the hills. From where does my help come? My help comes from the LORD, who made heaven and earth. He will not let your foot be moved; he who keeps you will not slumber. Behold, he who keeps Israel will neither slumber nor sleep. The LORD is your keeper; the LORD is your shade on your right hand. The sun shall not strike you by day, nor the moon by night. The LORD will keep you from all evil; he will keep your life. The LORD will keep your going out and your coming in from this time forth and forevermore. Lord, let that be true for my life!

In Yeshua's Name

Amen

Lord,

In this troubled time I turn to you, your word says what then shall we say to these things? If God is for us, who can be against us? He who did not spare his own Son but gave him up for us all, how will he not also with him graciously give us all things? Who shall bring any charge against God's elect? It is God who justifies. Who is to condemn? Christ Jesus is the one who died—more than that, who was raised—who is at the right hand of God, who indeed is interceding for us. Who shall separate us from the love of Christ? Shall tribulation, or distress, or persecution, or famine, or nakedness, or danger, or sword? As it is written, "For your sake we are being killed all the day long; we are regarded as sheep to be slaughtered." No, in all these things we are more than conquerors through him who loved us. For I am sure that neither death nor life, nor angels nor rulers, nor things present nor things to come, nor powers, nor height nor depth, nor anything else in all creation, will be able to separate us from the love of God in Christ Jesus our Lord. Thank You, I know you will see me through this time also.

In Yeshua's Name

Lord,

I know you hear my prayer, you will never leave or forsake us, right now I have troubles and I can't seem to stop thinking the worst. Help me see things positively. Your word says you will deliver me from my fears and if I look to you I will not be ashamed. You save out of all troubles. Let me be able to say like the scripture says the angel of the LORD encamps around those who fear him, and delivers them. Oh, taste and see that the LORD is good! Blessed is the man who takes refuge in him! Oh, fear the LORD, you his saints, for those who fear him have no lack! The young lions suffer want and hunger; but those who seek the LORD lack no good thing. Lord, let me lack no good thing.

In Yeshua's Name

Amen

Heavenly Father,

There is our foe, the adversary has made himself known in our lives. I have set the Lord always before me. Because he is at me right hand, I shall not be shaken. He says, fear not, stand firm and see the salvation of the Lord. Which he will work for you today. The Lord shall fight for you and you have only to be silent. Oh sing to the Lord a new song for he has done marvelous things! His right hand and his holy arm have worked salvation. May you always direct our lives I pray In Yeshua's Name.

Amen

Abba,

I can certainly say this is a troubled time for me. I look to you for help. I can say from my heart the Lord is my light and my salvation; whom shall I fear? The Lord is the stronghold of my life; of whom shall I be afraid? When evildoers assail me to eat up my flesh, my adversaries and foes, it is they who stumble and fall. One thing have I asked of the Lord, that will I seek after: that I may dwell the house of the Lord all the days of my life, to gaze upon the beauty of the Lord and inquire in his temple. For he will hide me in his shelter in the day of trouble; he will conceal me under the cover of his tent ; he will lift me high upon a rock. The Eternal God is my dwelling place and underneath the everlasting arms. And he thrust out the enemy from before me and said, destroy. I thank you Holy Father.

In Yeshua's Name

Amen

Heavenly Father,

Troubled times have come to us again and I can see the adversaries work. God is our refuge and strength in this time of trouble. Holy scripture says because you have made the Lord your dwelling place the Most High, who is my refuge no evil shall be allowed to befall you, Lord, I pray you make that reality in my life!

In Yeshua's Name

Amen

Lord,

I praise you awesome in power, Mighty God, King of kings and Lord of lords. In this time of pain and trouble I remember who I belong to Lord, my God, I am yours, faults and all, and where I am going, heaven is my home! I pray in Yeshua's Name.

Amen

Father,

I rejoice in the Lord for praise is fitting for the upright. Give thanks to the LORD with the harp! Sing to him to the accompaniment of a ten-stringed instrument! Sing to him a new song! Play skillfully as you shout out your praises to him! For the LORD's decrees are just, and everything he does is fair. Look, the LORD takes notice of his loyal followers, those who wait for him to demonstrate his faithfulness by saving their lives from death and sustaining them during times of famine. We wait for the LORD; he is our deliverer and shield. For our hearts rejoice in him, for we trust in his holy name. May we experience your faithfulness, O LORD, for we wait for you. I pray in Yeshua's Name.

Amen

Lord,

The Adversary will not have his way! In my troubles I look to you and speak The Word. Your Word says, Look, I have given you authority to tread on snakes and scorpions and on the full force of the enemy, and nothing will hurt you. As a result God highly exalted him and gave him the name that is above every name, so that at the name of Jesus every knee will bow—in heaven and on earth and under the earth—You give us charge to say, and I do to the adversary in my midst, I rebuke you, In Yeshua's Name you have to leave, Your Name, Yeshua, is above all names. Blessed be the Name of the Lord! I pray in Yeshua's Name.

Amen

Abba,

Your word says Clothe yourselves with the full armor of God so that you may be able to stand against the schemes of the devil. For our struggle is not against flesh and blood, but against the rulers, against the powers, against the world rulers of this darkness, against the spiritual forces of evil in the heavens. For this reason, take up the full armor of God so that you may be able to stand your ground on the evil day, and having done everything, to stand. This day and time truly is evil, death, destruction, sickness and pain. The only thing that will help us stand is The Word as he speaks to us. Yeshua said No one has ascended into heaven except the one who descended from heaven—the Son of Man. Just as Moses *lifted up the serpent in the wilderness*, so must the Son of Man be lifted up, so that everyone who believes in him may have eternal life. For this is the way God loved the world: He gave his one and only Son, so that everyone who believes in him will not perish but have eternal life. For God did not send his Son into the world to condemn the world, but that the world

should be saved through him. Your word is Truth and Life. Help us
O Lord in this troubled time. I pray in Yeshua's Name.
Amen

Holy Father,
I feel I am under attack from the enemy, the adversary, you said
No trial has overtaken you that is not faced by others. And God is
faithful: He will not let you be tried beyond what you are able to bear,
but with the trial will also provide a way out. It feels like more than
I can bear! Help me Holy Father! I speak Your Word "I have said
these things to you so that, united with me, you may have *shalom*.
In the world, you have trouble. But be brave! I have conquered the
world!" I so need Your shalom! But the Lord is faithful, and he will
strengthen you and protect you from the evil one. I do need your hand
of protection. The Lord will deliver me from every evil deed and will
bring me safely into his heavenly kingdom. To him be glory for ever
and ever! I pray in Yeshua's Name.
Amen.

Heavenly Father,
Thanks be to the LORD, for he is good, and his loyal love endures!
Let those delivered by the LORD speak out, those whom he delivered
from the power of the enemy, I was in trouble and you heard my cry.
Stay close beside me I pray, the adversary is still near, I know who
my help is! I will give thanks to the LORD for his loyal love, and for
the amazing things he has done for people! For he has satisfied those

who thirst, and those who hunger he has filled with food. Fill me I pray, I so need your loving touch! I pray in Yeshua's Name.
Amen

Abba,
I cry out to the LORD in my distress; deliver me from my troubles. Please heal and rescue me from the pits where I am trapped. I cried out to the LORD in my distress; there is none but you to help. Calm the storm, your word says they cried out to the LORD in their distress; he delivered them from their troubles. He sent them an assuring word and healed them; he rescued them from the pits where they were trapped. No one is holy like the LORD! There is no one other than you! There is no rock like our God! Break the bows of the mighty men, those that stumble gird with strength. I pray in Yeshua's Name.
Amen

Lord,
I delight in the law of the Lord; make me be like a tree planted by flowing streams; it yields its fruit at the proper time, and its leaves never fall off. LORD, how numerous are my enemies! Many attack me. Many say about me,"God will not deliver her." But you, LORD, are a shield that protects me; you are my glory and the one who restores me. To the LORD I cried out, and he answered me from his holy hill. I rested and slept; I awoke, for the LORD protects me. I am not afraid of the multitude of people who attack me from all directions. Rise up, LORD! Deliver me, my God! Yes, you will strike all my enemies

on the jaw; you will break the teeth of the wicked. The LORD delivers, show favor to your people. I pray in Yeshua's Name.
Amen

Lord,
I will be happy and rejoice in you! I will sing praises to you, O sovereign One! When my enemies turn back, they trip and are defeated before you. For you defended my just cause; from your throne you pronounced a just decision. You terrified the nations with your battle cry; you destroyed the wicked; you permanently wiped out all memory of them. The LORD rules forever; he reigns in a just manner. He judges the world fairly; he makes just legal decisions for the nations. Why does the wicked man reject God? He says to himself, "You will not hold me accountable." You have taken notice, for you always see one who inflicts pain and suffering. The unfortunate victim entrusts his cause to you; you deliver the fatherless. Break the arm of the wicked! Hold him accountable for his wicked deeds, which he thought you would not discover. Consequently the LORD provides safety for the oppressed; he provides safety in times of trouble. Your loyal followers trust in you, for you, LORD, do not abandon those who seek your help. Sing praises to the LORD, who rules in Zion! Tell the nations what he has done! For the one who takes revenge against murderers took notice of the oppressed; he did not overlook their cry for help when they prayed: "Have mercy on me, LORD! See how I am oppressed by those who hate me, O one who can snatch me away from the gates of death! Then I will tell about all your praiseworthy

acts; in the gates of the daughter of Zion I will rejoice because of your deliverance." The nations fell into the pit they had made; their feet were caught in the net they had hidden. The LORD revealed himself; he accomplished justice; the wicked were ensnared by their own actions. The wicked are turned back and sent to Sheol the Lord will reign, Your Kingdom is an everlasting Kingdom, in your mercy you save your people from death. Hallelujah! I pray in Yeshua's Name. Amen

Father,
Hear my plea for mercy when I cry out to you for help, when I lift my hands toward your holy temple! Do not drag me away with evil, with those who behave wickedly, who talk so friendly to their neighbors, while they plan to harm them! Pay them back for their evil deeds! Pay them back for what they do! Punish them! For they do not understand the LORD's actions, or the way he carries out justice. The LORD will permanently demolish them. The LORD deserves praise, for he has heard my plea for mercy! The LORD strengthens and protects me; I trust in him with all my heart. The LORD strengthens his people; Deliver your people! Care for them like a shepherd and carry them in your arms at all times! In Yeshua's Name
Amen

Father,
In you, O LORD, I have taken shelter! Never let me be humiliated! Vindicate me by rescuing me! Listen to me! Quickly deliver me! Be

my protector and refuge, a stronghold where I can be safe! For you are my high ridge and my stronghold; for the sake of your own reputation you lead me and guide me. You will free me from the net they hid for me, for you are my place of refuge. Into your hand I entrust my life; you will rescue me, O LORD, the faithful God. I hate those who serve worthless idols, but I trust in the LORD. I will be happy and rejoice in your faithfulness, because you notice my pain and you are aware of how distressed I am. You do not deliver me over to the power of the enemy; you enable me to stand in a wide open place. Have mercy on me, for I am in distress! My eyes grow dim from suffering. I have lost my strength. For I hear what so many are saying, the terrifying news that comes from every direction. When they plot together against me, they figure out how they can take my life. But I trust in you, O LORD! I declare, "You are my God!" You determine my destiny! Rescue me from the power of my enemies and those who chase me. Smile on your servant! Deliver me because of your faithfulness! O LORD, do not let me be humiliated, for I call out to you! How great is your favor, which you store up for your loyal followers! In plain sight of everyone you bestow it on those who take shelter in you. You hide them with you, The LORD deserves praise for he demonstrated his amazing faithfulness to me when I was besieged by enemies. I jumped to conclusions and said, "I am cut off from your presence!" But you heard my plea for mercy when I cried out to you for help. You are my hiding place; you protect me from distress. You surround me with shouts of joy, we will celebrate deliverance. I pray in Yeshua's Name. Amen

Abba, Father

Deliver me from evildoers! For look, they wait to ambush me; though I have done nothing wrong, they are anxious to attack. Spring into action and help me! Take notice of me! You are my source of strength! I will wait for you! For God is my refuge. As for me, I will sing about your strength; I will praise your loyal love in the morning. For you are my refuge and my place of shelter when I face trouble. You are my source of strength! I will sing praises to you! For God is my refuge, the God who loves me.

In Yeshua's Name

Amen

Lord,

Hide me from the conspiracy of the wicked, from the noisy crowd of the ones doing evil; who sharpen their tongue like a sword, and aim their arrows, deadly words, to shoot innocent people from ambushes. They shoot at them suddenly and fearlessly. They encourage themselves in evil plans. They talk about laying snares secretly. They say, "Who will see them?" They plot injustice, saying, "We have made a perfect plan!" But God will shoot at them. They will be suddenly struck down with an arrow. Their own tongues shall ruin them. The righteous shall be glad in the Name of the LORD, and shall take refuge in him. All the upright in heart shall praise him, not from what we have done, but by your cross you have made us right. You are greatly to be praised! I pray in Yeshua's Name.

Amen

Lord,

As smoke is driven away, so drive them away. As wax melts before the fire, so let the wicked perish at the presence of God. Blessed be the Lord, who daily bears our burdens, even the God who is our salvation. You are awesome, God, in your sanctuaries. The God of Israel gives strength and power to his people. Praise be to God! I pray in Yeshua's Name.

Amen

Father,

In you, O Lord, I have taken shelter! Never let me be humiliated! Vindicate me by rescuing me! Listen to me! Deliver me! Be my protector and refuge, a stronghold where I can be safe! For you are my high ridge and my stronghold. My God, rescue me from the power of the wicked, from the hand of the cruel oppressor! For you are my hope you are my secure shelter. I praise you constantly and speak of your splendor all day long. Do not reject me in my old age! When my strength fails, do not abandon me! For my enemies talk about me; those waiting for a chance to kill me plot my demise. They say, "God has abandoned him. Run and seize him, for there is no one who will rescue him!" God, don't be far from me. My God, hurry to help me. Let my accusers be disappointed and consumed. Let them be covered with disgrace and scorn who want to harm me. But I will always hope, and will add to all of your praise. My mouth will tell about your righteousness, and of your salvation all day, your righteousness also, God, reaches to the heavens; you have done great things. God, who is like you? You, who have shown us many and bitter troubles, you will let me live. You will bring us up again from the depths of the earth. Increase my honor, and comfort me again. My soul which you have redeemed, sings praise to you! I pray in Yeshua's Name.

Amen

Lord,

Remember me, O LORD, when you show favor to your people! Pay attention to me, when you deliver, so I may see the prosperity of your chosen ones, rejoice along with your nation, and boast along with the people who belong to you. O sovereign LORD, intervene on my behalf for the sake of your reputation! Because your loyal love is good, deliver me! For I am oppressed and needy, and my heart beats violently within me. You are just and merciful. You help the needy, help this needy person, Lord, for there is no one else who can save, no one like you, Lord. Mighty and awesome, wonderful, King of kings and Lord of lords. I pray in Yeshua's Name.

Amen

Lord,

O LORD, I cry out to you. Come quickly to me! Pay attention to me when I cry out to you! May you accept my prayer like incense, my uplifted hands like the evening offering! O LORD, place a guard on my mouth! Protect the opening of my lips! Do not let me have evil desires, or participate in sinful activities with those who behave wickedly. Surely I am looking to you, O sovereign LORD. In you I take shelter. Do not expose me to danger! Protect me from the snare they have laid for me, and the traps the evildoers have set. Let the wicked fall into their own nets, while I escape. I pray in Yeshua's Name. Amen

CHAPTER 5

Scriptures

Eagle's wings

Isaiah 40:21-31
New English Translation (NET)

21 Do you not know? Do you not hear? Has it not been told to you since the very beginning? Have you not understood from the time the earth's foundations were made? 22 He is the one who sits on the earth's horizon; its inhabitants are like grasshoppers before him. He is the one who stretches out the sky like a thin curtain, and spreads it out like a pitched tent. 23 He is the one who reduces rulers to nothing; he makes the earth's leaders insignificant. 24 Indeed, they are barely planted; yes, they are barely sown; yes, they barely take root in the earth, and then he blows on them, causing them to dry up, and the wind carries them away like straw. 25 "To whom can you compare me? Whom do I resemble?" says the Holy One. 26 Look up at the sky! Who created all these heavenly

lights? He is the one who leads out their ranks; he calls them all by name. Because of his absolute power and awesome strength, not one of them is missing. 27 Why do you say, Jacob, Why do you say, Israel, "The LORD is not aware of what is happening to me, My God is not concerned with my vindication"? 28 Do you not know? Have you not heard? The LORD is an eternal God, the Creator of the whole earth. He does not get tired or weary; there is no limit to his wisdom. 29 He gives strength to those who are tired; to the ones who lack power, he gives renewed energy. 30 Even youths get tired and weary; even strong young men clumsily stumble. 31 But those who wait for the LORD's help find renewed strength; they rise up as if they had eagles' wings, they run without growing weary, they walk without getting tired.

Deuteronomy 32:10-12
New English Translation (NET)

10 The LORD found him in a desolate land, in an empty wasteland where animals howl. He continually guarded him and taught him; he continually protected him like the pupil of his eye. 11 Like an eagle that stirs up its nest, that hovers over its young, so the LORD spread out his wings and took him, he lifted him up on his pinions. 12 The LORD alone was guiding him, no foreign god was with him.

Ruth 2:12
New English Translation (NET)

12 May the LORD reward your efforts! May your acts of kindness be repaid fully by the LORD God of Israel, from whom you have sought protection!"

Psalm 17:1-15
New English Translation (NET)
Psalm 17

A prayer of David.

1 LORD, consider my just cause! Pay attention to my cry for help! Listen to the prayer I sincerely offer! 2 Make a just decision on my behalf! Decide what is right! 3 You have scrutinized my inner motives; you have examined me during the night. You have carefully evaluated me, but you find no sin. I am determined I will say nothing sinful. 4 As for the actions of people— just as you have commanded, I have not followed in the footsteps of violent men. 5 I carefully obey your commands; I do not deviate from them. 6 I call to you for you will answer me, O God. Listen to me! Hear what I say! 7 Accomplish awesome, faithful deeds, you who powerfully deliver those who look to you for protection from their enemies. 8 Protect me as you would protect the pupil of your eye! Hide me in the shadow of your wings! 9 Protect me from the wicked men who attack me, my enemies who

crowd around me for the kill. 10 They are calloused; they speak arrogantly. 11 They attack me, now they surround me; they intend to throw me to the ground. 12 He is like a lion that wants to tear its prey to bits, like a young lion crouching in hidden places. 13 Rise up, LORD! Confront him! Knock him down! Use your sword to rescue me from the wicked man! 14 LORD, use your power to deliver me from these murderers, from the murderers of this world! They enjoy prosperity; you overwhelm them with the riches they desire. They have many children, and leave their wealth to their offspring. 15 As for me, because I am innocent I will see your face; when I awake you will reveal yourself to me

Psalm 36:5-7
New English Translation (NET)

5 O LORD, your loyal love reaches to the sky; your faithfulness to the clouds. 6 Your justice is like the highest mountains, your fairness like the deepest sea; you preserve mankind and the animal kingdom. 7 How precious is your loyal love, O God! The human race finds shelter under your wings.

Psalm 61:2-8
New English Translation (NET)

2 From the most remote place on earth I call out to you in my despair. Lead me up to a rocky summit where I can be safe! 3 Indeed, you

are my shelter, a strong tower that protects me from the enemy. 4 I will be a permanent guest in your home; I will find shelter in the protection of your wings. (Selah) 5 for you, O God, hear my vows; you grant me the reward that belongs to your loyal followers. 6 Give the king long life! Make his lifetime span several generations! 7 May he reign forever before God! Decree that your loyal love and faithfulness should protect him. 8 Then I will sing praises to your name continually, as I fulfill my vows day after day.

Psalm 63
New English Translation (NET)

A psalm of David, written when he was in the Judean wilderness.

1 O God, you are my God! I long for you! My soul thirsts for you, my flesh yearns for you, in a dry and parched land where there is no water. 2 Yes, in the sanctuary I have seen you, and witnessed your power and splendor. 3 Because experiencing your loyal love is better than life itself, my lips will praise you. 4 For this reason I will praise you while I live; in your name I will lift up my hands. 5 As if with choice meat you satisfy my soul. My mouth joyfully praises you, 6 whenever I remember you on my bed, and think about you during the nighttime hours. 7 For you are my deliverer; under your wings I rejoice. 8 My soul pursues you; your right hand upholds me. 9 Enemies seek to destroy my life, but they will descend into the depths of the earth. 10 Each one will be handed over to the sword;

their corpses will be eaten by jackals. 11 But the king will rejoice in God; everyone who takes oaths in his name will boast, for the mouths of those who speak lies will be shut up.

Malachi 4:1-3
New English Translation (NET)

4 (3:19) "For indeed the day is coming, burning like a furnace, and all the arrogant evildoers will be chaff. The coming day will burn them up," says the LORD who rules over all. "It will not leave even a root or branch. 2 But for you who respect my name, the sun of vindication will rise with healing wings, and you will skip about like calves released from the stall. 3 You will trample on the wicked, for they will be like ashes under the soles of your feet on the day which I am preparing," says the LORD who rules over all.

Restoration through the Lord

4 "Remember the law of my servant Moses, to whom at Mt. Sinai I gave rules and regulations for all Israel to obey. 5 Look, I will send you Elijah the prophet before the great and terrible day of the LORD arrives. 6 He will encourage fathers and their children to return to me, so that I will not come and strike the earth with judgment."

Strength

Exodus 15:2-3
New English Translation (NET)

2 The Lord is my strength and my song, and he has become my salvation. This is my God, and I will praise him, my father's God, and I will exalt him. 3 The Lord is a warrior, the Lord is his name.

Isaiah 40:28-31
New English Translation (NET)

28 Do you not know? Have you not heard? The Lord is an eternal God, the Creator of the whole earth. He does not get tired or weary; there is no limit to his wisdom. 29 He gives strength to those who are tired; to the ones who lack power, he gives renewed energy. 30 Even youths get tired and weary; even strong young men clumsily stumble. 31 But those who wait for the Lord's help find renewed strength; they rise up as if they had eagles' wings, they run without growing weary, they walk without getting tired.

Isaiah 58:10-11
New English Translation (NET)

10 You must actively help the hungry and feed the oppressed. Then your light will dispel the darkness, and your darkness will be

transformed into noonday. 11 The Lord will continually lead you; he will feed you even in parched regions. He will give you renewed strength, and you will be like a well-watered garden, like a spring that continually produces water.

1 Thessalonians 3:11-13
New English Translation (NET)

11 Now may God our Father himself and our Lord Jesus direct our way to you. 12 And may the Lord cause you to increase and abound in love for one another and for all, just as we do for you, 13 so that your hearts are strengthened in holiness to be blameless before our God and Father at the coming of our Lord Jesus with all his saints.

Philippians 4:13
King James Version (KJV)

13 I can do all things through Christ, who strengthens me.

Uplifting Scriptures

Luke 10:19
New English Translation (NET)

19 Look, I have given you authority to tread on snakes and scorpions and on the full force of the enemy, and nothing will hurt you.

2 Corinthians 10:4-5
New English Translation (NET)

4 for the weapons of our warfare are not human weapons, but are made powerful by God for tearing down strongholds. We tear down arguments 5 and every arrogant obstacle that is raised up against the knowledge of God, and we take every thought captive to make it obey Christ.

1 John 4:4
New English Translation (NET)

4 You are from God, little children, and have conquered them, because the one who is in you is greater than the one who is in the world.

1 John 3:8
New English Translation (NET)

8 The one who practices sin is of the devil, because the devil has been sinning from the beginning. For this purpose the Son of God was revealed: to destroy the works of the devil.

Exodus 14:13
New English Translation (NET)

13 Moses said to the people, "Do not fear! Stand firm and see the salvation of the Lord that he will provide for you today; for the Egyptians that you see today you will never, ever see again.

Psalm 35:1
New English Translation (NET)

1 O Lord, fight those who fight with me! Attack those who attack me!

Psalm 98:1-2
New English Translation (NET)

1 Sing to the Lord a new song, for he performs amazing deeds! His right hand and his mighty arm accomplish deliverance. 2 The Lord demonstrates his power to deliver; in the sight of the nations he reveals his justice.

Isaiah 35:4
New English Translation (NET)

4 Tell those who panic, "Be strong! Do not fear! Look, your God comes to avenge! With divine retribution he comes to deliver you."

Isaiah 59:19
New English Translation (NET)

19 In the west, people respect the Lord's reputation; in the east they recognize his splendor. For he comes like a rushing stream driven on by wind sent from the Lord.

2 Timothy 4:18
New English Translation (NET)

18 The Lord will deliver me from every evil deed and will bring me safely into his heavenly kingdom. To him be glory for ever and ever! Amen.

Hebrews 13:6
New English Translation (NET)

6 So we can say with confidence, *"The Lord is my helper, and I will not be afraid. What can people do to me?"*

Hebrews 2:14-15
New English Translation (NET)

14 Therefore, since the children share in flesh and blood, he likewise shared in their humanity, so that through death he could destroy the

one who holds the power of death (that is, the devil), 15 and set free those who were held in slavery all their lives by their fear of death.

Deuteronomy 33:27
New English Translation (NET)

27 The everlasting God is a refuge, and underneath you are his eternal arms; he has driven out enemies before you, and has said, "Destroy!"

Psalm 4
New English Translation (NET)
Psalm 4

For the music director, to be accompanied by stringed instruments; a psalm of David.

1 When I call out, answer me, O God who vindicates me! Though I am hemmed in, you will lead me into a wide, open place. Have mercy on me and respond to my prayer! 2 You men, how long will you try to turn my honor into shame? How long will you love what is worthless and search for what is deceptive? (Selah) 3 Realize that the LORD shows the godly special favor; the LORD responds when I cry out to him. 4 Tremble with fear and do not sin! Meditate as you lie in bed, and repent of your ways! (Selah) 5 Offer the prescribed sacrifices and trust in the LORD! 6 Many say, "Who can show us anything good?"

Smile upon us, LORD! 7 You make me happier than those who have abundant grain and wine. 8 I will lie down and sleep peacefully, for you, LORD, make me safe and secure.

Psalm 16
New English Translation (NET)

Psalm 16
A prayer of David.

1 Protect me, O God, for I have taken shelter in you. 2 I say to the LORD, "You are the Lord, my only source of well-being." 3 As for God's chosen people who are in the land, and the leading officials I admired so much— 4 their troubles multiply, they desire other gods. I will not pour out drink offerings of blood to their gods, nor will I make vows in the name of their gods. 5 LORD, you give me stability and prosperity; you make my future secure. 6 It is as if I have been given fertile fields or received a beautiful tract of land. 7 I will praise the LORD who guides me; yes, during the night I reflect and learn. 8 I constantly trust in the LORD; because he is at my right hand, I will not be upended. 9 So my heart rejoices and I am happy; my life is safe. 10 You will not abandon me to Sheol; you will not allow your faithful follower to see the Pit. 11 You lead me in the path of life; I experience absolute joy in your presence; you always give me sheer delight

Psalm 27
New English Translation (NET)

By David.

1 The LORD delivers and vindicates me! I fear no one! The LORD protects my life! I am afraid of no one! 2 When evil men attack me to devour my flesh, when my adversaries and enemies attack me, they stumble and fall. 3 Even when an army is deployed against me, I do not fear. Even when war is imminent, I remain confident. 4 I have asked the LORD for one thing— this is what I desire! I want to live in the LORD's house all the days of my life, so I can gaze at the splendor of the LORD and contemplate in his temple. 5 He will surely give me shelter in the day of danger; he will hide me in his home; he will place me on an inaccessible rocky summit. 6 Now I will triumph over my enemies who surround me! I will offer sacrifices in his dwelling place and shout for joy! I will sing praises to the LORD! 7 Hear me, O LORD, when I cry out! Have mercy on me and answer me! 8 My heart tells me to pray to you, and I do pray to you, O LORD. 9 Do not reject me! Do not push your servant away in anger! You are my deliverer! Do not forsake or abandon me, O God who vindicates me! 10 Even if my father and mother abandoned me, the LORD would take me in. 11 Teach me how you want me to live; lead me along a level path because of those who wait to ambush me! 12 Do not turn me over to my enemies, for false witnesses who want to destroy me testify against me. 13 Where would I be if I did not believe I would

experience the LORD's favor in the land of the living? 14 Rely on the LORD! Be strong and confident! Rely on the LORD

Psalm 34
New English Translation (NET)

Written by David, when he pretended to be insane before Abimelech, causing the king to send him away.

1 I will praise the LORD at all times; my mouth will continually praise him. 2 I will boast in the LORD; let the oppressed hear and rejoice! 3 Magnify the LORD with me! Let's praise his name together! 4 I sought the LORD's help and he answered me; he delivered me from all my fears. 5 Those who look to him for help are happy; their faces are not ashamed. 6 This oppressed man cried out and the LORD heard; he saved him from all his troubles. 7 The LORD's angel camps around the LORD's loyal followers and delivers them. 8 Taste and see that the LORD is good! How blessed is the one who takes shelter in him! 9 Remain loyal to the LORD, you chosen people of his, for his loyal followers lack nothing! 10 Even young lions sometimes lack food and are hungry, but those who seek the LORD lack no good thing. 11 Come children! Listen to me! I will teach you what it means to fear the LORD. 12 Do you want to really live? Would you love to live a long, happy life? 13 Then make sure you don't speak evil words or use deceptive speech! 14 Turn away from evil and do what is right! Strive for peace and promote it! 15 The LORD pays attention to the

godly and hears their cry for help. 16 But the Lord opposes evildoers and wipes out all memory of them from the earth. 17 The godly cry out and the Lord hears; he saves them from all their troubles. 18 The Lord is near the brokenhearted; he delivers those who are discouraged. 19 The godly face many dangers, but the Lord saves them from each one of them. 20 He protects all his bones; not one of them is broken. 21 Evil people self-destruct; those who hate the godly are punished. 22 The Lord rescues his servants; all who take shelter in him escape punishment.

Psalm 46
New English Translation (NET)

For the music director; by the Korahites; according to the *alamoth* style; a song.(Alamoth - to be sung by a soprano or women's voice)

1 God is our strong refuge; he is truly our helper in times of trouble. 2 For this reason we do not fear when the earth shakes, and the mountains tumble into the depths of the sea, 3 when its waves crash and foam, and the mountains shake before the surging sea. (Selah) 4 The river's channels bring joy to the city of God, the special, holy dwelling place of the sovereign One. 5 God lives within it, it cannot be moved. God rescues it at the break of dawn. 6 Nations are in uproar, kingdoms are overthrown. God gives a shout, the earth dissolves. 7 The Lord who commands armies is on our side!

The God of Jacob is our protector! (Selah) 8 Come! Witness the exploits of the LORD, who brings devastation to the earth! 9 He brings an end to wars throughout the earth; he shatters the bow and breaks the spear; he burns the shields with fire. 10 He says, "Stop your striving and recognize that I am God! I will be exalted over the nations! I will be exalted over the earth!" 11 The LORD who commands armies is on our side! The God of Jacob is our protector! (Selah)

Psalm 91
New English Translation (NET)

1 As for you, the one who lives in the shelter of the sovereign One, and resides in the protective shadow of the mighty king— 2 I say this about the LORD, my shelter and my stronghold, my God in whom I trust— 3 he will certainly rescue you from the snare of the hunter and from the destructive plague. 4 He will shelter you with his wings; you will find safety under his wings. His faithfulness is like a shield or a protective wall. 5 You need not fear the terrors of the night, the arrow that flies by day, 6 the plague that comes in the darkness, or the disease that comes at noon. 7 Though a thousand may fall beside you, and a multitude on your right side, it will not reach you. 8 Certainly you will see it with your very own eyes— you will see the wicked paid back. 9 For you have taken refuge in the LORD, my shelter, the sovereign One. 10 No harm will overtake you; no illness will come near your home. 11 For he will order his angels to protect you in all

you do. 12 They will lift you up in their hands, so you will not slip and fall on a stone. 13 You will subdue a lion and a snake; you will trample underfoot a young lion and a serpent. 14 The LORD says, "Because he is devoted to me, I will deliver him; I will protect him because he is loyal to me. 15 When he calls out to me, I will answer him. I will be with him when he is in trouble; I will rescue him and bring him honor. 16 I will satisfy him with long life, and will let him see my salvation.

Proverbs 1:33
New English Translation (NET)

33 But the one who listens to me will live in security, and will be at ease from the dread of harm.

Proverbs 3:24-26
New English Translation (NET)

24 When you lie down you will not be filled with fear; when you lie down your sleep will be pleasant. 25 You will not be afraid of sudden disaster, or when destruction overtakes the wicked; 26 for the LORD will be the source of your confidence, and he will guard your foot from being caught in a trap.

Proverbs 14:26-27
New English Translation (NET)

26 In the fear of the LORD one has strong confidence, and it will be a refuge for his children. 27 The fear of the LORD is like a life-giving fountain, to turn people from deadly snares.

Proverbs 18:10
New English Translation (NET)

10 The name of the LORD is like a strong tower; the righteous person runs to it and is set safely on high.

Proverbs 21:31
New English Translation (NET)

31 A horse is prepared for the day of battle, but the victory is from the LORD.

Proverbs 30:5
New English Translation (NET)

5 Every word of God is purified; he is like a shield for those who take refuge in him.

Matthew 7:7
New English Translation (NET)
Ask, Seek, Knock

7 "Ask and it will be given to you; seek and you will find; knock and the door will be opened for you.

John 14:27
New English Translation (NET)

27 "Peace I leave with you; my peace I give to you; I do not give it to you as the world does. Do not let your hearts be distressed or lacking in courage.

John 15:7
New English Translation (NET)

7 If you remain in me and my words remain in you, ask whatever you want, and it will be done for you.

Isaiah 41:10-11
New English Translation (NET)

10 Don't be afraid, for I am with you! Don't be frightened, for I am your God! I strengthen you— yes, I help you— yes, I uphold you with my saving right hand! 11 Look, all who were angry at you will

be ashamed and humiliated; your adversaries will be reduced to nothing and perish.

Romans 8
World English Bible (WEB)

There is therefore now no condemnation to those who are in Christ Jesus, who don't walk according to the flesh, but according to the Spirit. 2 For the law of the Spirit of life in Christ Jesus made me free from the law of sin and of death. 3 For what the law couldn't do, in that it was weak through the flesh, God did, sending his own Son in the likeness of sinful flesh and for sin, he condemned sin in the flesh; 4 that the ordinance of the law might be fulfilled in us, who walk not after the flesh, but after the Spirit. 5 For those who live according to the flesh set their minds on the things of the flesh, but those who live according to the Spirit, the things of the Spirit. 6 For the mind of the flesh is death, but the mind of the Spirit is life and peace; 7 because the mind of the flesh is hostile towards God; for it is not subject to God's law, neither indeed can it be. 8 Those who are in the flesh can't please God. 9 But you are not in the flesh but in the Spirit, if it is so that the Spirit of God dwells in you. But if any man doesn't have the Spirit of Christ, he is not his. 10 If Christ is in you, the body is dead because of sin, but the spirit is alive because of righteousness. 11 But if the Spirit of him who raised up Jesus from the dead dwells in you, he who raised up Christ Jesus from the dead will also give life to your mortal bodies through his

Spirit who dwells in you. 12 So then, brothers, we are debtors, not to the flesh, to live after the flesh. 13 For if you live after the flesh, you must die; but if by the Spirit you put to death the deeds of the body, you will live. 14 For as many as are led by the Spirit of God, these are children of God. 15 For you didn't receive the spirit of bondage again to fear, but you received the Spirit of adoption, by whom we cry, "Abba! Father!" 16 The Spirit himself testifies with our spirit that we are children of God; 17 and if children, then heirs; heirs of God, and joint heirs with Christ; if indeed we suffer with him, that we may also be glorified with him. 18For I consider that the sufferings of this present time are not worthy to be compared with the glory which will be revealed toward us. 19For the creation waits with eager expectation for the children of God to be revealed. 20 For the creation was subjected to vanity, not of its own will, but because of him who subjected it, in hope 21 that the creation itself also will be delivered from the bondage of decay into the liberty of the glory of the children of God. 22 For we know that the whole creation groans and travails in pain together until now. 23 Not only so, but ourselves also, who have the first fruits of the Spirit, even we ourselves groan within ourselves, waiting for adoption, the redemption of our body. 24 For we were saved in hope, but hope that is seen is not hope. For who hopes for that which he sees? 25 But if we hope for that which we don't see, we wait for it with patience. 26 In the same way, the Spirit also helps our weaknesses, for we don't know how to pray as we ought. But the Spirit himself makes intercession for us with groanings which can't be uttered. 27 He who searches the hearts knows what is on the Spirit's mind, because he makes intercession for the saints according to God. 28 We know that all things work together for good for those who love God, to those who are called according to his purpose. 29 For whom he foreknew, he also predestined to be conformed to the image of his Son, that he might be the firstborn among many brothers. 30 Whom he predestined, those he also called. Whom he called, those he also justified. Whom he justified, those he also glorified. 31 What then shall we say about these things? If God is for us, who can be against us? 32 He who didn't spare his own Son, but delivered him up for us all, how would he not also with him freely give us all things? 33 Who could bring a charge against God's chosen ones? It is God who justifies. 34 Who is he who condemns? It is Christ who died, yes rather, who was raised from the dead, who is at the right hand of God, who also makes intercession for us. 35 Who shall separate us from the love of Christ? Could oppression, or anguish, or persecution, or famine, or nakedness, or peril, or sword? 36 Even as it is written, "For your sake we are killed all day long. We were accounted as sheep for the slaughter." 37 No, in all these things, we are more than conquerors through him who loved us. 38 For I am persuaded, that neither death, nor life, nor angels, nor principalities, nor things present, nor things to come, nor powers, 39 nor height, nor depth, nor any other created thing, will be able to separate us from the love of God, which is in Christ Jesus our Lord.

Isaiah 53
New English Translation (NET)

53 Who would have believed what we just heard? When was the LORD's power revealed through him? 2 He sprouted up like a twig before God, like a root out of parched soil; he had no stately form or majesty that might catch our attention, no special appearance that we should want to follow him. 3 He was despised and rejected by people, one who experienced pain and was acquainted with illness; people hid their faces from him; he was despised, and we considered him insignificant. 4 But he lifted up our illnesses, he carried our pain; even though we thought he was being punished, attacked by God, and afflicted for something he had done. 5 He was wounded because of our rebellious deeds, crushed because of our sins; he endured punishment that made us well; because of his wounds we have been healed. 6 All of us had wandered off like sheep; each of us had strayed off on his own path, but the LORD caused the sin of all of us to attack him. 7 He was treated harshly and afflicted, but he did not even open his mouth. Like a lamb led to the slaughtering block, like a sheep silent before her shearers, he did not even open his mouth. 8 He was led away after an unjust trial— but who even cared? Indeed, he was cut off from the land of the living; because of the rebellion of his own people he was wounded. 9 They intended to bury him with criminals, but he ended up in a rich man's tomb, because he had committed no violent deeds, nor had he spoken deceitfully. 10 Though the LORD desired to crush him and make him ill, once restitution is made, he

will see descendants and enjoy long life, and the LORD's purpose will be accomplished through him. 11 Having suffered, he will reflect on his work, he will be satisfied when he understands what he has done. "My servant will acquit many, for he carried their sins. 12 So I will assign him a portion with the multitudes, he will divide the spoils of victory with the powerful, because he willingly submitted to death and was numbered with the rebels, when he lifted up the sin of many and intervened on behalf of the rebels."

2 Timothy 1:7
New English Translation (NET)

7 For God did not give us a Spirit of fear but of power and love and self-control.

Thoughts on Job

Even though Job felt abandoned by GOD, and in a way he was, but not really, because it was God who saw Job through his suffering. He will never leave you or forsake you. Job never abandoned his faith. Devil accused saying if only you strike him with… he will abandon his faith, for a while blessings seemed far from Job, but God in his mercy, blessed him more at the end of his life than the first. With what I went through I can identify myself in that. Just like when we heard that the Job time for me was over, David and I hear we are going to have something good come our way, and here is that old accuser step in the way again thinking he could stop GOD, He didn't stop GOD, God just went right through! Hallelujah!

P.S. These words are for you. God wants you to know that. you can Say these scriptures out loud or pray them, God loves to hear from his children, especially from The Word, Yeshua, Jesus.